Gazzotti
Vehlmann

alone

3 The Clan of the Shark

9th CINEBOOK
The 9th Art Publisher

- My thanks to Géraldine.
Fabien

- For Lili.
Caroline & Ralph

Colours: Caroline & Ralph

Original title: Seuls – Le Clan du requin

Original edition: © Dupuis, 2008 by Gazzotti & Vehlmann
www.dupuis.com
All rights reserved

English translation: © 2015 Cinebook Ltd

Translator: Jerome Saincantin
Lettering and text layout: Design Amorandi
Printed in Spain by EGEDSA

This edition first published in Great Britain in 2015 by
Cinebook Ltd
56 Beech Avenue
Canterbury, Kent
CT4 7TA
www.cinebook.com

A CIP catalogue record for this book
is available from the British Library

ISBN 978-1-84918-250-8

COME ON, IT WAS JUST A THEORY!

MORE TINNED FOOD? ARGH, I WANT AN APPLE!

I HAVE TO ADMIT, I'M STARTING TO MISS FRESH FRUIT AND VEGETABLES!

DON'T LEAVE ME LIKE THIS... I'M HUNGRY!

SERVES YOU RIGHT FOR SAYING YOU'RE GOD!

THAT'S NOT WHAT I SAID! MY THEORY WAS THAT 'I MIGHT BE THE ONLY SENTIENT BEING IN THE UNIVERSE AND...'

...AND EVERYTHING AROUND YOU IS A FIGMENT OF YOUR IMAGINATION: THE WORLD, US, THE VANISHING... SUUURE!

WHAT? FROM MY POINT OF VIEW, HOW CAN I BE SURE THAT YOU REALLY EXIST?! THE ONLY THING I KNOW FOR CERTAIN IS WHAT I FEEL!

WELL, BY TYING YOU UP, I JUST PROVED TO YOU THAT I'M REAL!

OR NOT... MAYBE IT'S JUST A NEW TWIST HATCHED BY MY SUPER-POWERFUL BRAIN TO SPICE UP MY EXISTENCE.

GIMME A FORK, CAMILLE. I'M GOING TO SPICE UP HIS EXISTENCE A BIT MORE.

OK, OK, I TAKE IT BACK.

YOU EVIL PRODUCT OF MY IMAGINATION!

WHATCHA DOING? CAN I COME WITH YOU?

I SAW SMOKE. I WANT TO CHECK THAT IT'S NOT ANOTHER FIRE STARTING.

YOU KNOW, TERRY, YOU NEED TO GIVE ME BACK MY BED AT SOME POINT.

AFTER ALL, YOU'RE THE ONE LEILA BUILT THE SMALL BED FOR. I'M TOO BIG FOR IT — MY FEET DANGLE OFF THE END. IT SUCKS.

BUT... I DON'T WANNA SLEEP OVER THE STAIRS... I'M SCAAAARED!

WHAT IF THERE ARE MONSTERS?! THE DOOR... WELL, IT DOESN'T EVEN LOCK PROPERLY!

WELL, THEN, WE'LL PUT A STRONGER DOOR, THAT'S ALL.

HOW CAN ANYONE BE SUCH A SCAREDY...

DOGS! A PACK OF DOGS! UNTIE IVAN, QUIIIIIICK!

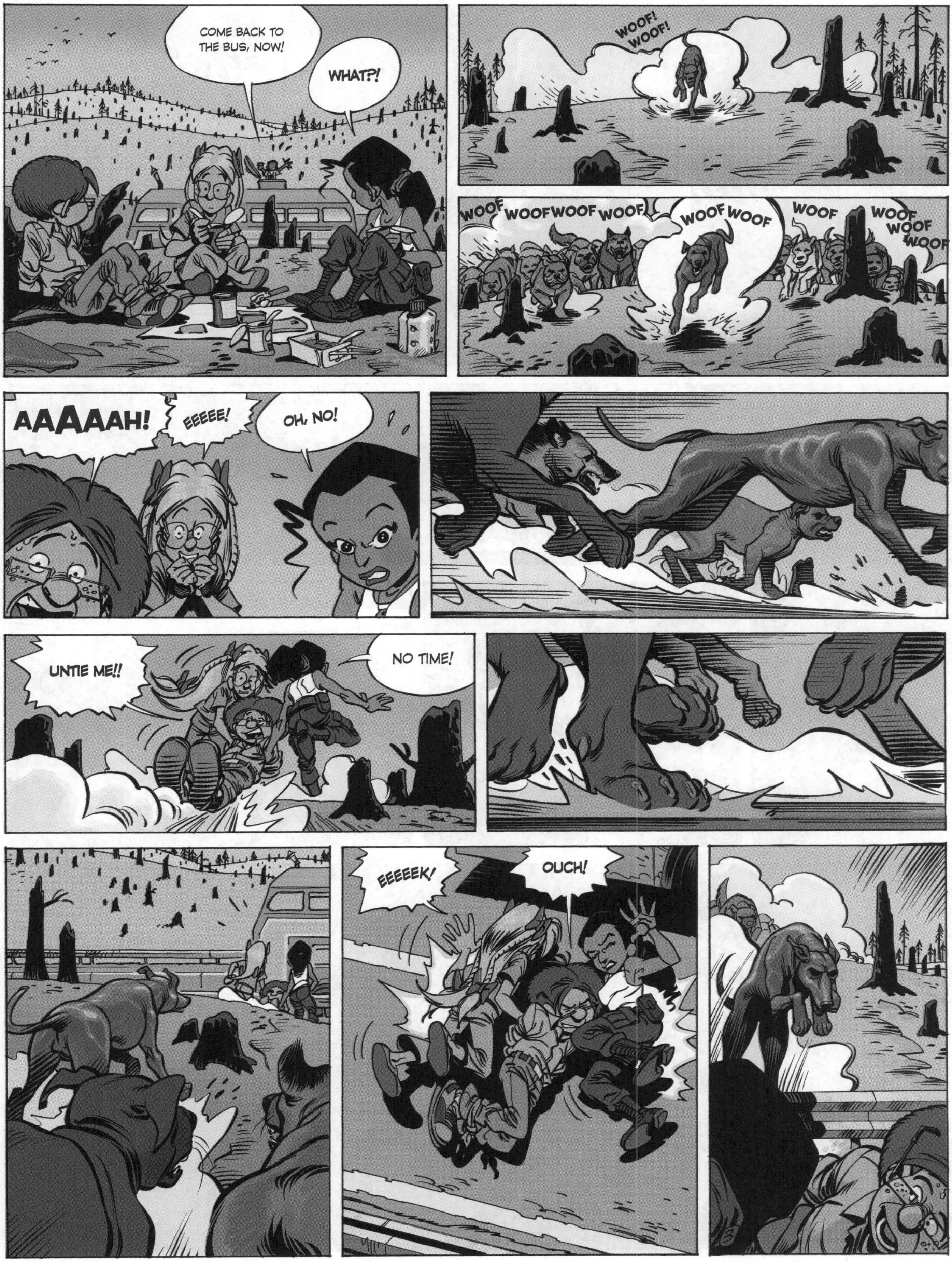
COME BACK TO THE BUS, NOW!
WHAT?!
WOOF! WOOF!
WOOF WOOFWOOF WOOF
WOOF WOOF
WOOF
WOOF WOOF WOOF
AAAAAH!
EEEEE!
OH, NO!
UNTIE ME!!
NO TIME!
EEEEEK!
OUCH!

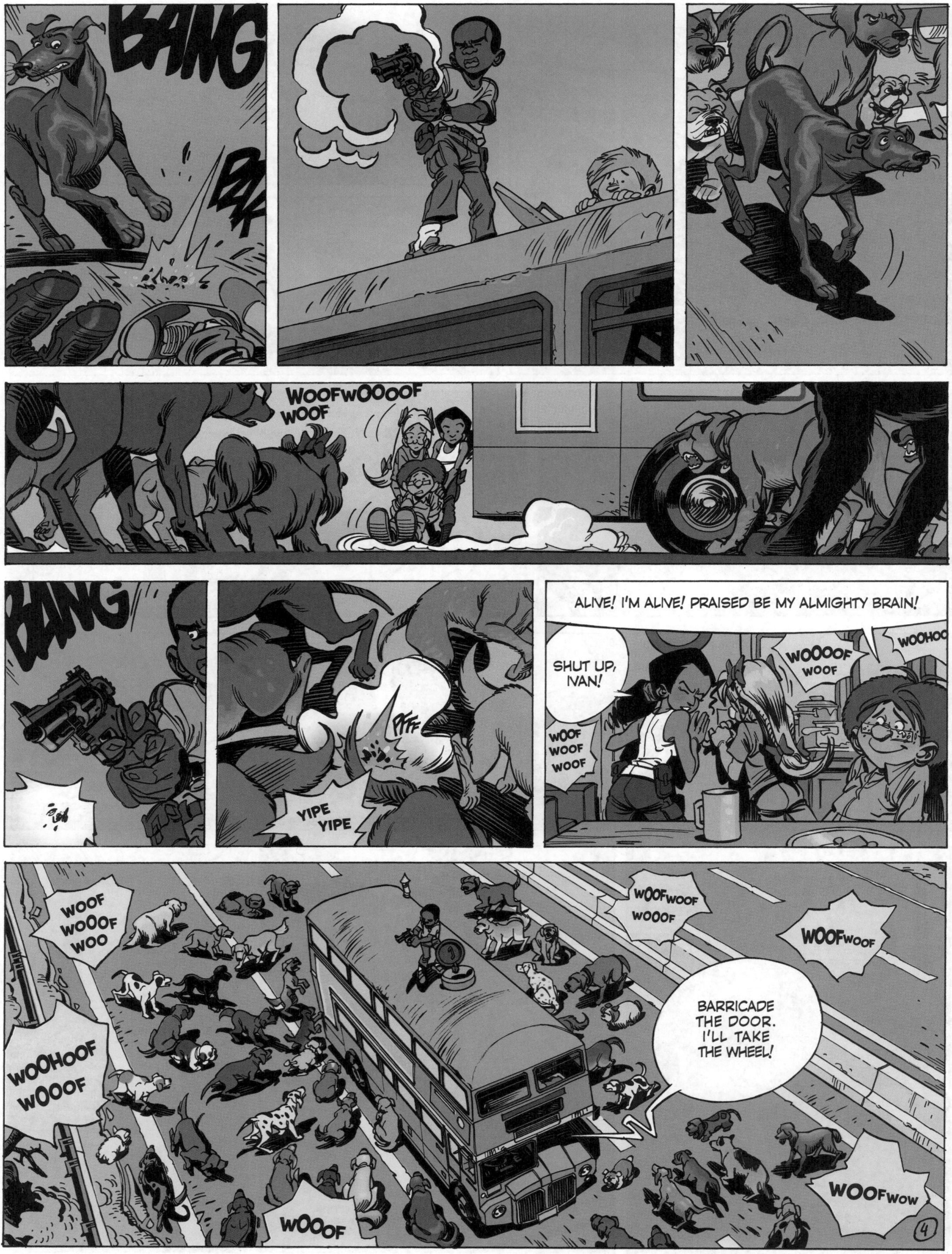
BANG
BZK
WOOFWOOOOF
WOOF
BANG
PFFF
YIPE
YIPE
ALIVE! I'M ALIVE! PRAISED BE MY ALMIGHTY BRAIN!
SHUT UP, IVAN!
WOOF
WOOF
WOOF
WOOOOF
WOOF
WOOHOO
WOOF
WOOOF
WOO
WOOFWOOF
WOOOF
WOOFWOOF
BARRICADE THE DOOR. I'LL TAKE THE WHEEL!
WOOHOOF
WOOOF
WOOOF
WOOFWOW
4

MORNING, LEILA...

DON'T TELL ME YOU DROVE ALL NIGHT?

I LOST THEM FOR A WHILE AND I SLEPT A BIT, BUT THEY WOKE ME UP... THEY WERE SCRATCHING AT THE BUS'S DOORS...

MY FATHER TOLD ME THAT DOGS THAT GO FERAL ARE WORSE THAN WOLVES, BECAUSE THEY AREN'T AFRAID OF PEOPLE.

THE SCARY THING IS THAT WE'RE ALMOST OUT OF PETROL.

BOMBOM

WHAT IS IT, DODZI?

ON THE RIGHT! LOOK!

OTHER CHILDREN!

TAKE THE NEXT EXIT!

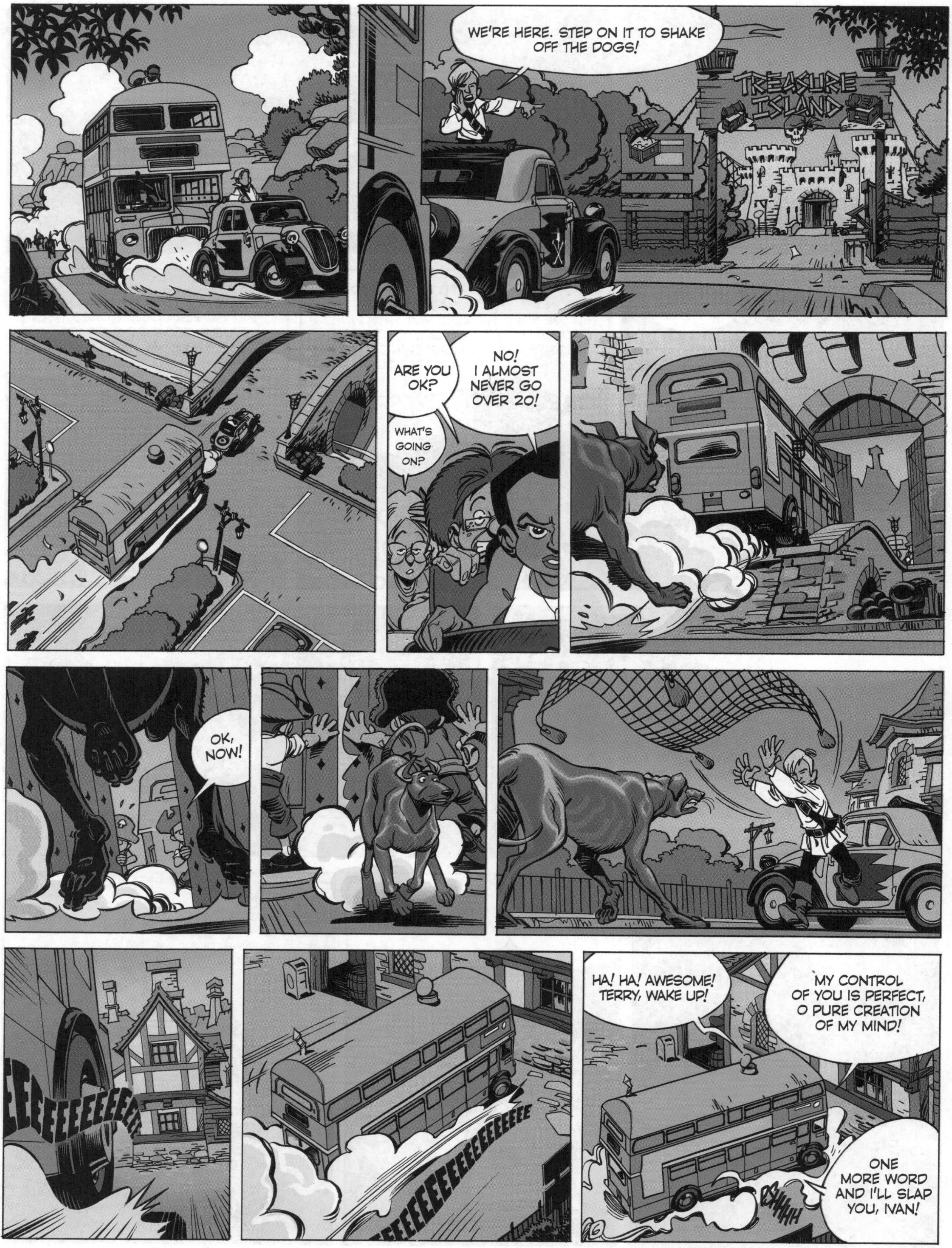
WE'RE HERE. STEP ON IT TO SHAKE OFF THE DOGS!
TREASURE ISLAND
ARE YOU OK?
NO! I ALMOST NEVER GO OVER 20!
WHAT'S GOING ON?
OK, NOW!
EEEEEEEEEEEE
EEEEEEEEEEEEEEEEE
HA! HA! AWESOME! TERRY, WAKE UP!
MY CONTROL OF YOU IS PERFECT, O PURE CREATION OF MY MIND!
SHHHH
ONE MORE WORD AND I'LL SLAP YOU, IVAN!

YEAAAAAAAAAAAH!

OH! LOOK, LOTS OF BOYS!

WHERE ARE WE?

WELCOME, NEW GUYS!

HA! HA!

HEY, THERE ARE GIRLS, TOO!

THIS IS OUR PLACE. D'YOU LIKE IT?

YOU LIVE HERE?

YEAH! IT'S BRILLIANT — YOU'LL SEE!

THERE'S WATER ALL AROUND THE PARK. THE DOGS CAN'T GET TO US!

OH, YEAH! TREASURE ISLAND, THAT AMUSEMENT PARK I SAW ON THE TV NEWS ONCE!

AND THAT'S SAUL, OUR LEADER!

WOOF WOOF WOOWOOW WOOF

HMMM!

BRRM!

WELCOME TO THE CLAN OF THE SHARK.

WOF WOW WOF WO

AND LOOK WHAT WE HAVE HERE!

WOOF WOOF WOOF WOOF

YEAAAAAAH!

TO THE TANK!

WHAT ARE THEY GOING...?

COME WITH US — YOU'LL SEE!

IN THE TANK! IN THE TANK!

WOOF WOOF WOOF

IN THE TANK!

SAUL... STRANGE NAME. WHERE'S HE FROM?

HE'S FROM LONDON.

HIS DAD'S MATTHEW BARRIE. YOU KNOW, THE MILLIONAIRE. HE'S THE ONE WHO BUILT THE PARK.

THE WHOLE FAMILY MOVED HERE AWHILE AGO. BUT, THEY ALL VANISHED TOO.

OH, YES, I REMEMBER THAT GUY! HE'S ONE OF THE ONLY PEOPLE IN THE WORLD WHO MANAGED TO KEEP A GREAT WHITE SHARK IN CAPTIVITY!

IT WAS SAUL WHO FOUND US, ONE GROUP AFTER THE OTHER, AND BROUGHT US BACK HERE!

BUT, WHAT IS HE...?

HE'S GONNA THROW IT INTO THE SHARK TANK! IT'LL BE A CARNAGE!

WHAT?!... THAT'S HORRIBLE! HE CAN'T DO THAT TO THAT POOR DOG!

WELL, WE'VE GOT TO FEED THE SHARK, DON'T WE? OR **HE'LL** DIE.

HUH? BUT I... OH... ER. SHOOT!?

COULDN'T YOU GIVE IT SOME CORNFLAKES INSTEAD?

DUUNNN DUNNN!... IT'S *JAWS* TIME!

I... I CAN'T WATCH THIS!

THERE IT IS!

IT COMES AS SOON AS IT FEELS MOVEMENT IN THE WATER NOW!

THAT'S WHAT HAPPENS TO MUTTS THAT TRY TO EAT US!

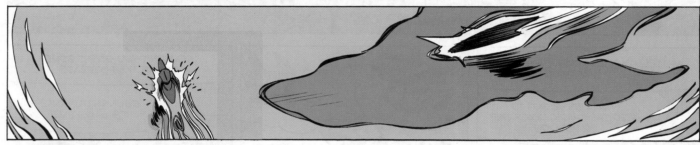

IT'S ATTACKING!

WHERE? I CAN'T SEE!

YOU SEE IT?

OooOooH!

...COME ON, WHERE'S THE EXIT?!

SHOOT, I WENT TOO FAR DOWN...

?!

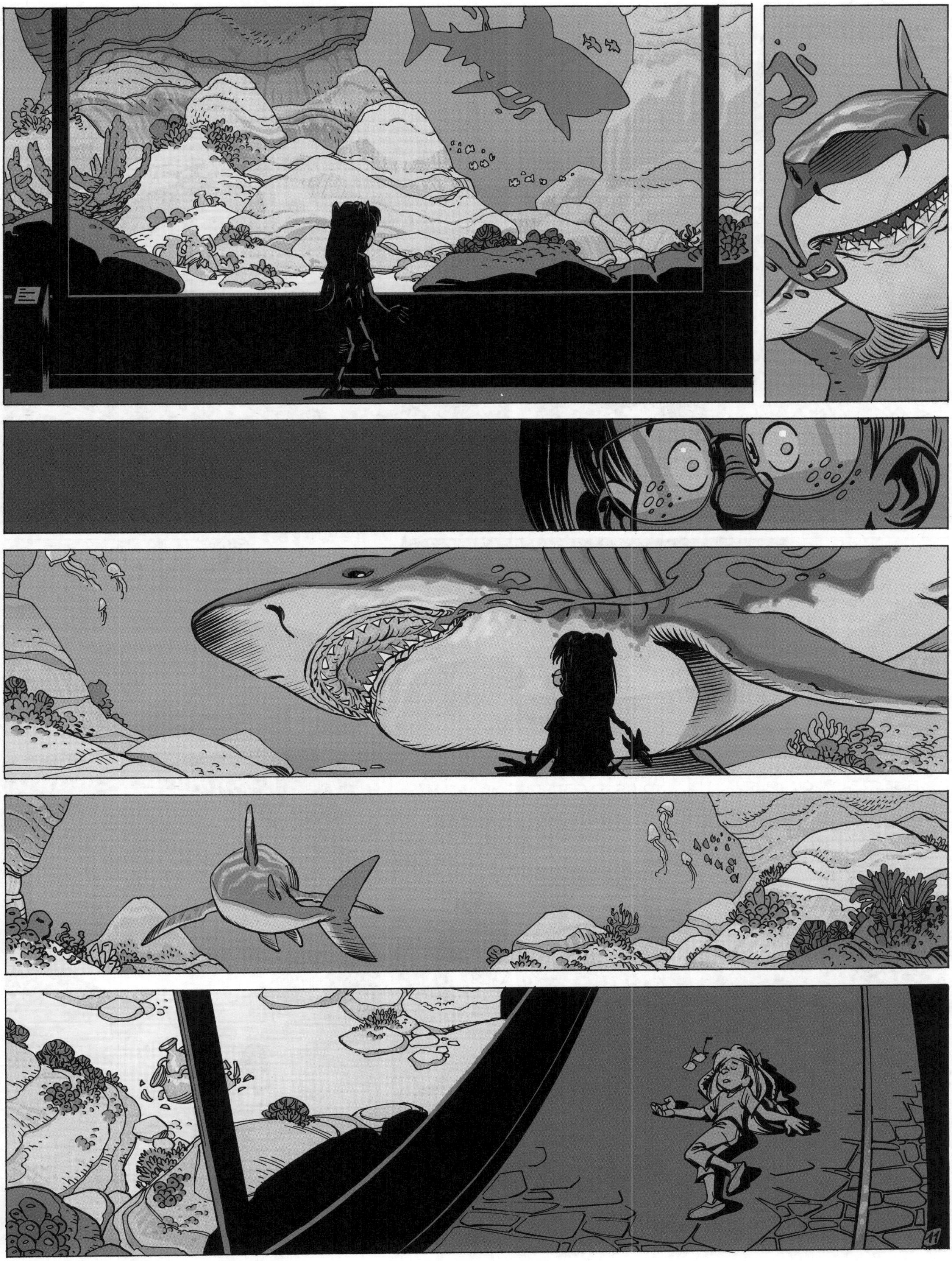
11

WHEEEEEE!...

YIPPEEE!...

HEY, ARE YOU COMING, YOU WUSSIES? THE WATER'S GREAT!

...BUT, THE TOWNS WE VISITED WERE JUST AS EMPTY AS OURS, AND SOME HAD EVEN COMPLETELY BURNED DOWN!

DO YOU WANT SOMETHING ELSE TO EAT? YOU'RE STILL A BIT PALE.

THANKS, DODZI, I'M FEELING BETTER.

YEAH, IT HAPPENED THE SAME WAY TO US, EXCEPT THAT ME AND MY FRIENDS KNEW EACH OTHER BEFORE THE VANISHING. WE WERE IN THE SAME CLASS.

♥ IS THAT SO?

I WOKE UP SUDDENLY AROUND 10 PM. IT WAS LIKE THERE HAD BEEN A BIG NOISE!... AFTER THAT, I GOT OUT OF BED, AND THERE WAS NO ONE LEFT IN THE VILLAGE.

♥ IS THAT SO?

AROUND 10 PM... ARE YOU SURE?

IT WAS BEFORE 11 O'CLOCK, ANYWAY, AND THE SAME FOR MY FRIENDS. WHY?

IT DOESN'T FIT WITH WHAT WE THOUGHT. FOR US, IT SEEMS LIKE IT HAPPENED AFTER MIDNIGHT. HOW IS THAT POSSIBLE?

MAYBE IT STARTED WITH YOU GUYS AND THEN TRAVELLED TO OUR TOWN?

LIKE A SORT OF WAVE...

...MAYBE IT CAME FROM THE OCEAN.

WHAT YOU'RE SAYING IS...

YES?

WHAT YOU'RE SAYING, ER...

GUYS, THIS IS BONEHEAD. HE'S JUST WEIRD — HE NEVER FINISHES HIS SENTENCES!

AND HE WETS HIS BEH-ED! HEEHEEHEE!

ARE YOU COMING OR WHAT?! OR ELSE YOU'RE JUST A BUNCH OF BUMHEADS! HAHAHA!!

...WE'VE GOT TIME, DON'T WE?

YES, BUT AFTERWARDS WE ALL HAVE TO GATHER ON THE MAIN SQUARE. SAUL WANTS TO HOLD THE CEREMONY.

THE... ER... THE CEREMONY FOR WHAT?

YOU'LL FIND OUT LATER... EVERYONE IN THE WATER!!

BROBROLOBRO

THIS WAS THE PARK'S GALLOWS, BEFORE.

THEY USED TO HAVE FAKE PIRATE HANGINGS!... SAUL TURNED IT INTO A STAGE FOR SPECIAL OCCASIONS.

LOVELY...

AND WHAT'S TODAY'S SPECIAL, THEN?

YOU'LL SEE!

FRIENDS... WITH THE NEWEST ARRIVALS, THERE ARE NOW ENOUGH OF US FOR THE RITUAL I TOLD YOU ABOUT.

LET'S BEGIN THE WEDDINGS CEREMONY!

YEAAAAAAAAAAAH!

OH!

WHAT?!

WHAT THE HECK?

SAUL THINKS WE SHOULD LIVE LIKE WE DID BEFORE THE VANISHING. SO, HE WANTS THERE TO BE COUPLES AND EVERYTHING.

I'M GOING TO DRAW THE NAMES.

HE'S ... GOING TO MAKE US MARRY EACH OTHER?

SERIOUSLY?... AREN'T THERE MORE IMPORTANT THINGS TO DO? WE HAVE TO FIND OUR PARENTS!

SAUL SAYS IT'S BEST FOR THE CLAN.

THE FIRST NAME IS ... CAMILLE!

HUH? WHAT?! IT'S ALREADY **MY WEDDING?!**

SHE'LL BE WITH...

...ME!

SAUL

16

CAMILLE! YOU DON'T HAVE TO AGREE! HEY!

...DO SIT DOWN. I HAVE TO CONTINUE THE DRAWING.

YES-YES-OK-AS-YOU-SAY!!

I DON'T UNDERSTAND! ARE THEY GOING TO HANG CAMILLE?

THE NEXT ONE IS ... DODZI!

YOU GUYS ARE GETTING ALL THE FUN! HAHA!

WHO'S GOING TO MARRY...

...OH?

IVAN!

HAHAHA! HEHEHEHEHE! HAHAHA

?!!

SORRY, WE NEEDED THE SAME NUMBER OF NAMES IN EACH BARREL ... AND THERE ARE MORE BOYS THAN GIRLS!

IT'S RIGGED... HE DID IT ON PURPOSE!

THIS IS RUBBISH!

HA! HA! WE'LL LET YOU DECIDE WHO GETS TO WEAR THE DRESS!

DODZI!

WHOA, THERE... WHERE D'YOU THINK YOU'RE GOING?

OUT OF MY WAY, DUMBO... GIVE ME SOME PETROL, AND THEN I'M NOT STAYING ANOTHER SECOND IN YOUR STUPID PARK.

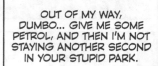

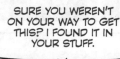

SURE YOU WEREN'T ON YOUR WAY TO GET THIS? I FOUND IT IN YOUR STUFF.

YOU'RE GONNA HAVE TO TELL US WHAT YOU WERE PLANNING TO DO HERE WITH IT.

WHERE DID THEY TAKE THEM?

CAMILLE MUST BE STAYING WITH SAUL, IN THE ADMINISTRATION BUILDINGS. DODZI... I DON'T KNOW. HE HAS SOME EXPLAINING TO DO: HE SCARED EVERYONE WITH HIS GUN.

ZOE! I TOLD YOU IT WASN'T AGAINST YOU! IT WAS ... JUST IN CASE!

WELL, IF THAT'S SO, SAUL WILL RELEASE HIM QUICKLY.

I **REALLY** HAVE TO WEAR THIS DRESS? I THOUGHT IT WAS A JOKE!

WE ... HAVE TO OBEY SAUL... IT'S THE LAW OF THE CLAN.

M'YEAH... Y'KNOW, I MIGHT BE ABLE TO MAKE SOMETHING OUT OF IT.

YOU GUYS DID EVERYTHING HERE? IT'S A PRETTY COOL HOME, ACTUALLY.

IT'S JUST A PITY I'M MARRIED TO THE MIDGET.

I DIDN'T WANT TO BE MARRIED TO YOU! YOU'VE GOT STINKY HAIR!

AND I DON'T WANT BONEHEAD TO SLEEP HERE EITHER! I WANT DODZI!

...WHOA, HEY, LET'S START WITH DROPPING THAT STUPID NICKNAME.

WHAT'S YOUR ACTUAL NAME?

ER... AN... ANTON.

19

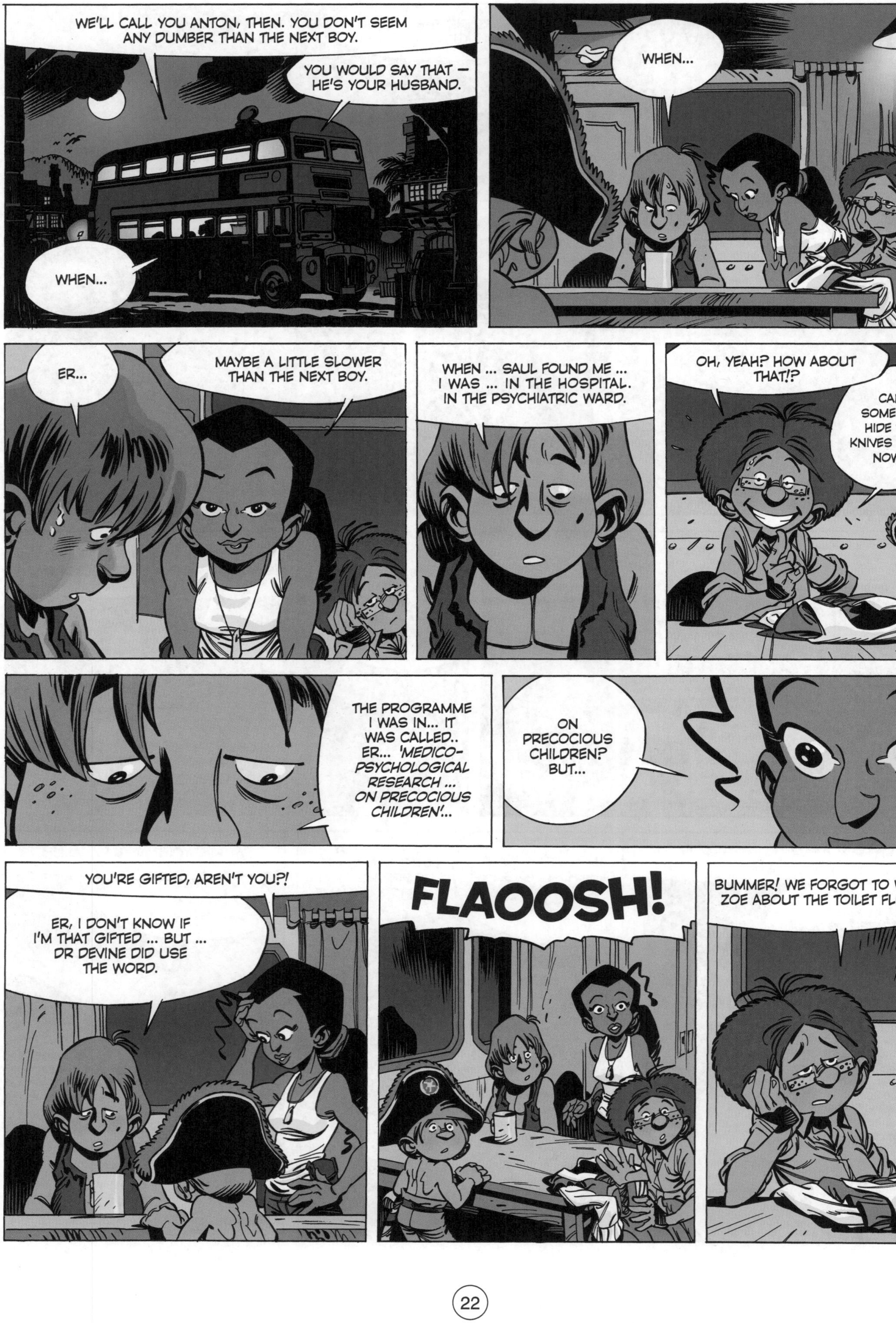
WE'LL CALL YOU ANTON, THEN. YOU DON'T SEEM ANY DUMBER THAN THE NEXT BOY.
YOU WOULD SAY THAT — HE'S YOUR HUSBAND.
WHEN...
WHEN...
ER...
MAYBE A LITTLE SLOWER THAN THE NEXT BOY.
WHEN ... SAUL FOUND ME ... I WAS ... IN THE HOSPITAL. IN THE PSYCHIATRIC WARD.
OH, YEAH? HOW ABOUT THAT!?
CAN SOMEONE HIDE THE KNIVES RIGHT NOW?
THE PROGRAMME I WAS IN... IT WAS CALLED.. ER... 'MEDICO-PSYCHOLOGICAL RESEARCH ... ON PRECOCIOUS CHILDREN'...
ON PRECOCIOUS CHILDREN? BUT...
YOU'RE GIFTED, AREN'T YOU?!
ER, I DON'T KNOW IF I'M THAT GIFTED ... BUT ... DR DEVINE DID USE THE WORD.
FLAOOSH!
BUMMER! WE FORGOT TO WARN ZOE ABOUT THE TOILET FLUSH.
20

ER, ZOE, DON'T USE THE TOILETS. THEY DON'T WORK TOO WELL YET!

THANKS FOR THE TIP.

WHAT'S YOUR GIFT? SHOW US A TRICK!

HE'S NOT A TRAINED MONKEY, TERRY!

ER, I DON'T DO ANYTHING SPECIAL... I JUST LOVE READING... BUT, THERE AREN'T ANY BOOKS IN THE PARK, AND I'M BORED.

SAUL CALLED ME BONEHEAD FOR FUN... SO, THE OTHERS... WHEN I SAY SOMETHING THEY DON'T UNDERSTAND, THEY SAY I'M THE DUMB ONE.

I DON'T THINK SAUL CALLED YOU THAT 'FOR FUN', ANTON.

HE DID IT ON PURPOSE BECAUSE HE DOESN'T WANT ANY RIVALS. NOT YOU, NOT DODZI... NO ONE.

HE'S SMART. HE KNOWS HOW TO WIN PEOPLE OVER BY MAKING THEM LAUGH. I USED TO DO THE SAME IN SCHOOL!

ER... ARE YOU GUYS DONE TALKING?

I'M TIRED. ARE YOU COMING TO BED?

SAUL'S A GOOD LEADER, BUT SOMETIMES HE ALSO SCARES US A LITTLE.

EARLY ON, SOMEONE JOKED: 'I DARE YOU TO SWIM ACROSS THE SHARK'S TANK'. AND, JUST LIKE THAT, SAUL DIVED IN AND SWAM STRAIGHT ACROSS.

THE SHARK CAME PRETTY CLOSE... LIKE, 20 YARDS OR SO! BUT, HE DIDN'T CARE. WHEN HE CAME OUT, HE JUST ASKED IF ANYONE ELSE DARED.

I'D DARE!

...WOW. THAT'S PRETTY GUTSY.

HE'S... NOT AFRAID OF ANYTHING... THAT'S WHY NO ONE HAS THE GUTS TO SAY ANYTHING WHEN HE GOES TOO FAR...

YEAH, WELL, DODZI'S EVEN TOUGHER. WE THINK HE STRAIGHT-OUT KILLED HIS STEPFATHER TO STOP HIM FROM BEATING HIM... CAN YOU IMAGINE?

ER, LEILA, I'M NOT SURE WE SHOULD TELL ANYONE ...

WOW!...

DODZI WON'T LET SAUL PUSH HIM AROUND. HE'D BETTER WATCH OUT.

I JUST HOPE SAUL WON'T HURT DODZI AND CAMILLE.

THE HITLER YOUTH

HITLER: A BIOGRAPHY

NATIONAL SOCIALISM

HISTORY OF THE LUFTWAFFE 40-45

BATTLE OF STALINGRAD

IT'S A PERIOD OF HISTORY I FIND FASCINATING.

REALLY?... ER... THAT'S UNUSUAL!

HEY, ABOUT DODZI... YOU WON'T BE TOO HARD ON HIM, WILL YOU? HE'S MY FRIEND!

WE'LL SEE.

I'LL LEAVE THIS HERE, IN CASE YOU WANT TO TRY IT ON. IT'S FROM THE PARK'S COSTUME COLLECTION.

YOU CAN SLEEP IN MY BED... I WON'T BOTHER YOU.

BUT, LEAVE THE LIGHTS ON, ALL RIGHT?

TING TING

ARE YOU COMING FISHING WITH ME?

NAH! SAUL WANTS ME TO CHECK ON THE FENCES!

HEY, THE NEW GUYS ARE COMING!

HAHA! CAN'T WAIT TO SEE FOUR-EYES IN HIS PRETTY DRESS! WHAT A LOSER!

TINGTING TING

BUH?

WHERE'S DODZI?

PRETTY COOL, ISN'T IT? ALL I NEED IS A PIRATE HAT AND I'LL LOOK JUST AWESOME.

YEAH, BUT... BUT, YOU'RE WEARING A DRESS, SO IT'S LAME!

...CAN YOU DO THAT? SAUL SAID THAT...

SAUL SAID THAT I SHOULD WEAR THE DRESS. I'M WEARING THE DRESS.

IF I MAY?

WE WANT TO SEE DODZI. WHERE IS HE?

SAUL WILL TELL YOU... HEY, YOU'RE NOT WEARING YOUR DRESS YET?

ALSO, YOU'RE SUPPOSED TO HELP US MAKE BREAKFAST FOR THE OTHERS.

SORRY, I DON'T DO COOKING. I'M FINE WITH HELPING OUT, BUT I'M MORE OF A TINKERING GIRL.

BUT, ALL THE GIRLS HELP WITH THE COOKING HERE! OR WE DO THE LAUNDRY!

BESIDES, TINKERING IS FOR BOYS! YOU'RE TALKING NONSENSE!

IS THAT ANOTHER OF SAUL'S STUPID RULES?

BUT ... IT WAS ALREADY THAT WAY BEFORE THE VANISHING, SILLY!

LOOK AT TOY CATALOGUES! YOU FIND TOOLS IN THE BOYS' SECTION AND COOKWARE IN THE GIRLS'! ISN'T THAT PROOF?

LISTEN, GIRLY, IF YOU WANT TO MODEL YOUR LIFE AFTER DUMB MAGAZINES, THAT'S YOUR PROBLEM. I DO WHAT I WANT.

...HEY! HURRY UP! I THINK I FOUND DODZI!!!

25

♪ DAH DIDIH DAAAAAA DAHDAH DIIIII! ♪

♪ DAH DIDIH DAAAAAAH DIHDIHDIH DIIIII! ♪

DODZI!

HEY! STAY BACK!

♪ DIHDIHDIH DAAAADAHDIH... ♪

HE HAS TO SERVE HIS SENTENCE!

THIS IS SICK! CUT HIM DOWN RIGHT NOW! YOU CAN'T TIE UP DODZI!

♪ DIHDIH DAH ♪

OH, NO... POOR DODZI! ...

WHAT IS IT, ANTON?

♪ DIHDIHDAAA ♪

I... I WAS TIED TO THE MERRY-GO-ROUND ONCE... WHEN SAUL PUNISHED ME...

♪ DIHDIH DAAA ♪

I WAS ON IT FOR TWO HOURS... THE MUSIC ... GAVE ME A HORRIBLE MIGRAINE... AND I... I THREW UP A WHOLE BUNCH...

♪ DIHDIH DAAA DIHDIH DADAAH ♪

HOW LONG HAS HE BEEN ON THERE?

♪ DIHDIHDIH... DAAA ♪

WELL... HE SPENT THE NIGHT...

♪ DIHDIH DAAA ♪

THE WHOLE NIGHT?! BUT, YOU... YOU DIDN'T GIVE HIM A CHANCE TO EXPLAIN?

DIHDIHDIH DAAA

YOU'RE MONSTERS!

IT'S JUST A MERRY-GO-ROUND! IT CAN'T KILL HIM!

HE SHOULDN'T HAVE BROUGHT A GUN! SERVES HIM RIGHT!

DIHDIH DIHDAAA

WHOA, RELAX! I THINK THE WISE COUNSEL OF *Mister Lady* IS URGENTLY NEEDED HERE!

DIHDIHDIH DAAA

Mister Lady! HAHAHA!!

DEFENDER OF THE WEAK AND THE HELPLESS, AT YOUR SERVICE! WHAT'S THE PROBLEM, THEN?

DIHDIHDIHDAAA

YOUR FRIEND'S BEING A PAIN!

TRUE. I'LL GRANT YOU THAT SHE'S GOT A BIT OF A TEMPER.

CAN'T QUESTION SAUL'S ORDERS OR WE'LL PAY FOR IT!

DIH

DIH BRANK

HEYY!

SHE BROKE IT!

SAUL'S GONNA KILL US!

GET HER!

TERRY, RUN TO THE BUS AND LOCK YOURSELF IN, OK?

WHERE ARE YOU GOING?

TO TRY AND HELP LEILA!

27

ARE YOU AWAKE?

...YES.

THE DRESS SUITS YOU.

...CAMILLE, WE HAVE TO... TO MAKE LOVE.

...WHAT?!

WE HAVE TO MAKE BABIES, YOU UNDERSTAND?... IT'S FOR THE CLAN.

ARE YOU CRAZY?!... WHAT ARE YOU TALKING ABOUT? WE'RE TOO YOUNG!!

I'M ALREADY 11.

MAYBE, BUT I'M ONLY EIGHT!

WELL, EIGHT AND A HALF, BUT STILL!

HOW CAN YOU EVEN THINK THAT...?!

BEDOOP BEDO-OP BEDOOP

CHARLIE?

OK, HAVE DODZI BROUGHT TO MY PLACE... I'LL HELP YOU FIND LEILA.

YOU'VE GOTTA BE KIDDING!... HOW DO THEY ALWAYS KNOW WHERE I AM?!

CRAP! CRAP! CRAP! CRAP!

SHE'S HEADING YOUR WAY. JUST WAIT AND GRAB HER...

BEDO-OP BEDO-OP DOOP DOOP...

...IVAN! WHAT ARE YOU...?

LEILA, STOP RIGHT NOW! THEY'RE JUST AHEAD OF YOU!

YES, YES, I KNOW THEY'RE EVERYWHERE!... GO THROUGH THE FENCE TO YOUR LEFT!

FOLLOW ME!

OK, KEEP GOING... NOW, TURN RIGHT!

HEY, WHAT...?!

ARE YOU SURE THERE'S NO OTHER WAY OUT?

SHE'S HERE!

OK, I SEE.

UNNH! HE'S MUCH HEAVIER THAN ME!

GOTCHA, LITTLE MERMAID! HAHA!

GAAAH! LET GO OF ME!

RUH' BLL' UGLLB!

MFFUG?

WE'RE GOING TOO FAAAAST!

OH, NO!

PAK PAK

I SAID LET GO OF ME!

HEY?! OW! OUCH!

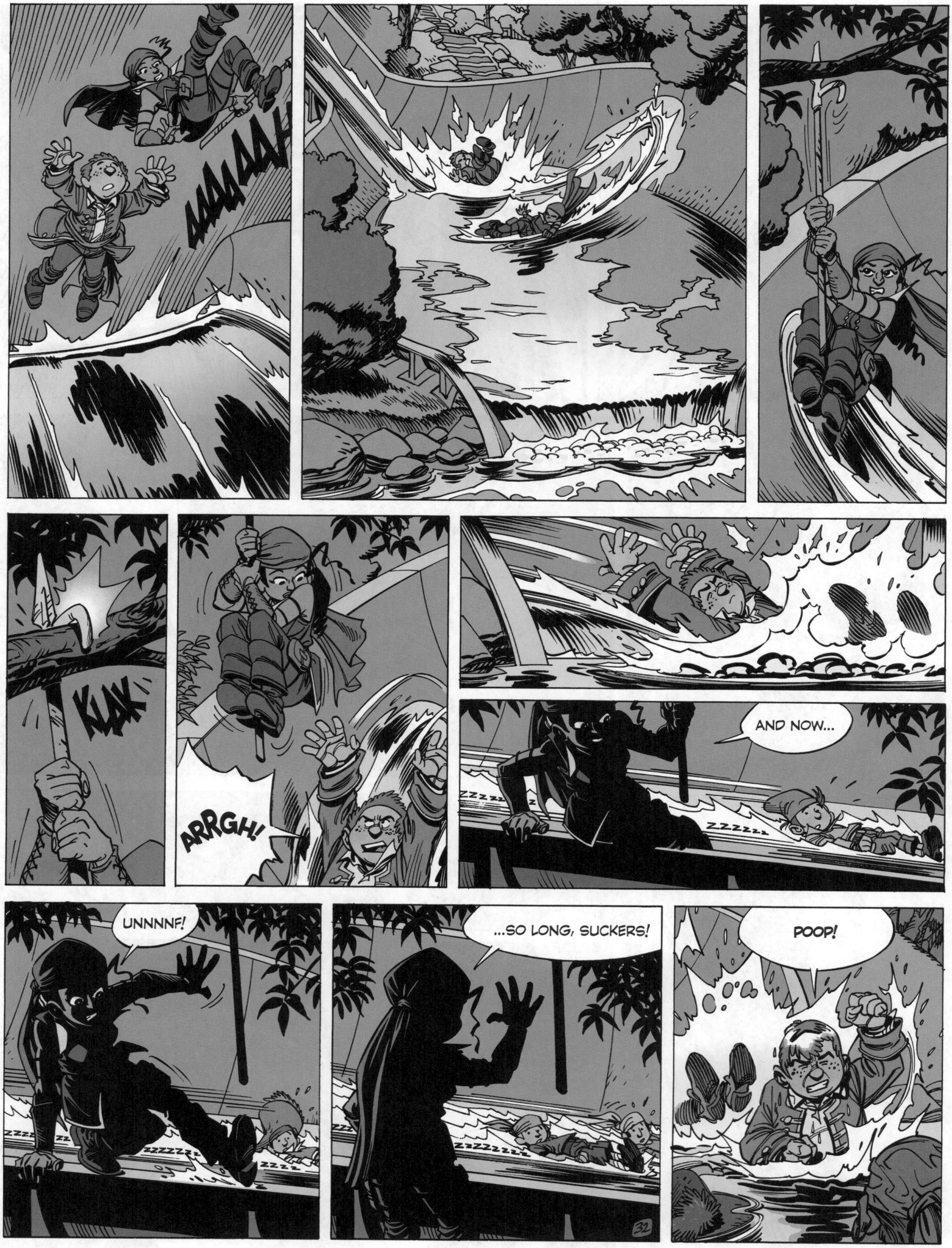
AAAAAAAH
KLAK
ARRGH!
AND NOW...
UNNNNF!
...SO LONG, SUCKERS!
POOP!

WELL DONE, LEILA!

THAT SAID, I'VE GOT TO GET DOWN FROM HERE, NOW...

WHAT ARE WE GOING TO DO?

I DON'T KNOW... WE SHOULD FIND DODZI, AND TAKE BACK THE BUS, AND... AND ALSO FIND SOME PETROL...

WE'VE GOT OUR WORK CUT OUT FOR US, THEN... WE DON'T EVEN KNOW WHERE DODZI IS!

AND THE PARK IS HUGE...

33

SAUL'S GONNA GET PAYBACK FOR SURE ...

I HEAR THE OTHER ONE'S DISAPPEARED TOO, THE ONE WITH THE DRESS.

MISTER LADY?

YOU'LL NEVER GUESS WHAT ZOE TOLD ME ABOUT DODZI!

WE LOST THEM... I'M SORRY.

IT'S TOO DARK NOW. COME BACK.

...YOU SHOULDN'T BE OUT AT NIGHT.

...

...NO... NO! IT'S GOING TO GET ME!...

SAUL?... SAUL, ARE YOU OK?

DADDY, PLEASE!... DADDY, WHERE ARE YOU?

CAMILLE?...

IT'S OK, SAUL, IT WAS JUST A BAD DREAM.

...HOLD ME TIGHT.

...I HAVE... I HAVE TO FIX THINGS, CAMILLE!

35

TING
TING

...THEY SAY THAT, FOR SAMURAIS, A WARRIOR'S WEAPON WAS HIS SOUL.

SO, THIS THING'S YOUR SOUL.

...DID YOU KILL YOUR STEPFATHER WITH IT?

WHO TOLD YOU THAT?

RUMOURS... YOU KILLED HIM IN HIS SLEEP, IS THAT IT? OTHERWISE, HE REALLY WAS A LOSER, GETTING BLOWN AWAY BY A KID.

MY FATHER COULDN'T STAND LOSERS. HE WAS STRONG.

YOU KNOW, I HAVE THIS MEMORY OF HIM. WE WERE DOING 120 MILES PER HOUR ON THE MOTORWAY WHEN A WASP LANDED ON HIS ARM.

HE STAYED COOL AS ICE. HE KNEW IF HE MOVED, HE MIGHT LOSE CONTROL OF THE CAR.

THE WASP STUNG HIM ANYWAY. MAYBE BECAUSE MY MOTHER WAS WAVING HER ARMS AROUND, I DON'T KNOW... WELL, HE DIDN'T MOVE AN INCH. HE JUST WAITED FOR IT TO LEAVE.

CAN YOU IMAGINE? THAT'S HOW HE WAS, MY FATHER... AND I WILL BE STRONG, TOO, AND SAVE THE CLAN.

BUT, I DON'T MEAN YOU ANY HARM! I...

SINCE YOU GOT HERE, YOU'VE RUINED EVERYTHING!

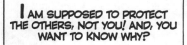

I AM SUPPOSED TO PROTECT THE OTHERS, NOT YOU! AND, YOU WANT TO KNOW WHY?

BECAUSE I'M THE ONLY ONE WHO REMEMBERS WHAT HAPPENED!

YOU... YOU REMEMBER?! BUT... WHAT HAPPENED?

IT WAS SO DARK I COULDN'T SEE A THING... IT WAS HORRIBLE!

...WE'RE NEARING THE END, DODZI... THE END OF EVERYTHING AROUND US.

WE'LL NEVER SEE OUR PARENTS AGAIN.

BUT, MAYBE NOT EVERYONE IS DOOMED... MAYBE THE STRONGEST CAN FIND A WAY TO MAKE IT.

...YOU'RE LYING. I BET YOU DON'T REMEMBER ANYTHING.

I DON'T NEED TO CONVINCE YOU, DODZI... ANYWAY, WE'LL DO THIS BY THE BOOK.

CHILDREN OF THE CLAN!

I ASK ALL OF YOU TO COME TO THE TANK.

DODZI IS WAITING FOR YOU.

WE GOTTA GO!

D'YOU THINK IT MIGHT BE A TRAP?

OF COURSE IT'S A TRAP. WE DON'T HAVE A CHOICE, THOUGH.

CAN YOU IMAGINE WHAT THAT WEIRDO MIGHT DO TO DODZI IF WE DON'T GO?

38

I'M GLAD TO SEE YOU AGAIN.

LISTEN TO ME!

SINCE DODZI AND THE OTHERS SHOWED UP, SOME OF YOU HAVE LOST YOUR TRUST IN ME.

BUT, WE HAVE TO STAY UNITED! IT'S THE ONLY THING THAT MATTERS TO ME!

DO YOU REMEMBER THE FIRST TIME I SWAM ACROSS THIS TANK BEFORE YOU?

DOES ANYONE ELSE HERE THINK HE CAN DO IT TOO? IF HE SUCCEEDS, HE'LL REPLACE ME AS LEADER!

I CAN...? MAYBE?

THAT'D BE CRAZY!

NOW THAT THE SHARK'S USED TO BEING FED HERE... THERE'S NO WAY!

THAT CREEP!

GO ON! LET HIM STEP FORWARD NOW, OR ACCEPT ME AS BOSS!

FINE... IF THAT'S HOW YOU WANT IT.

DODZI, NO! DON'T WALK INTO HIS TRAP!

NO-O-O-O!

WE HAVE TO HELP HIM!

THIS WAY! WE CAN GO DOWN TO THE SMALLER TANK!

IT'S COMING!

LOOK OUT, DODZI!

T... TOO FAR!

THE SHARK'S GOING AFTER DODZI! HE'LL NEVER MAKE IT!

HE... HE HAS TO STOP MOVING — THAT ATTRACTS IT!

I'LL GET ITS ATTENTION!

DODZI! STOP SWIMMING! DON'T MOVE!

STOP SWIMMING?

THIS WAY, YOU STUPID FISH! COME ON!

SPLASH SPLASH SPLASH SPL...

DODZI! FLOAT ON YOUR BACK!... YOU GOTTA BREATHE DEEP AND LOCK YOUR LUNGS! JUST LIKE IN SWIMMING CLASS!

HHHHHH!

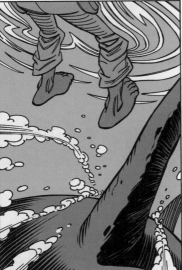

41

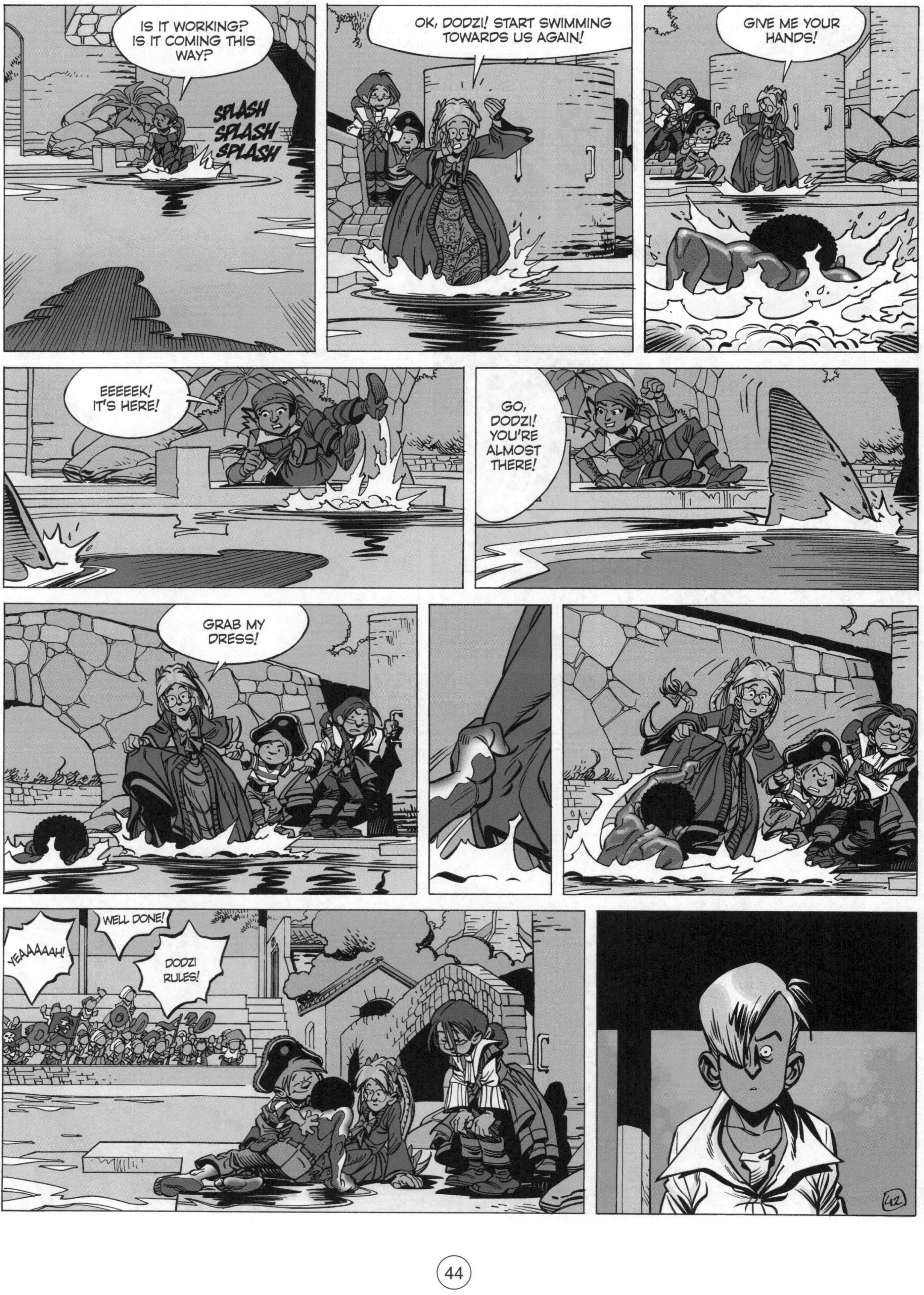
IS IT WORKING? IS IT COMING THIS WAY?
SPLASH SPLASH SPLASH
OK, DODZI! START SWIMMING TOWARDS US AGAIN!
GIVE ME YOUR HANDS!
EEEEEK! IT'S HERE!
GO, DODZI! YOU'RE ALMOST THERE!
GRAB MY DRESS!
YEAAAAAH!
WELL DONE!
DODZI RULES!
42

TH... THANKS

YOU'RE A NUTJOB, YOU KNOW THAT? COMPLETELY MAD TO DO THIS!

HHHHH... DADDY!... IT'S NOT MY FAULT... THEY CHEATED!...

I... I'M SCARED, DADDY!... ISN'T THERE ANOTHER WAY?...

YOU ROCKED, DODZI!

HEY, GOOD THING YOU HAD YOUR FRIENDS, RIGHT?!

IT'S NOT OVER!

THE CHALLENGE IS NOT OVER.

I'LL SHOW YOU THAT I'M STILL THE LEADER!

AND, WHEN WE'RE FACE TO FACE, DODZI, I SWEAR I'LL KILL YOU!

SAUL! NO! YOU DON'T HAVE TO DO THIS!

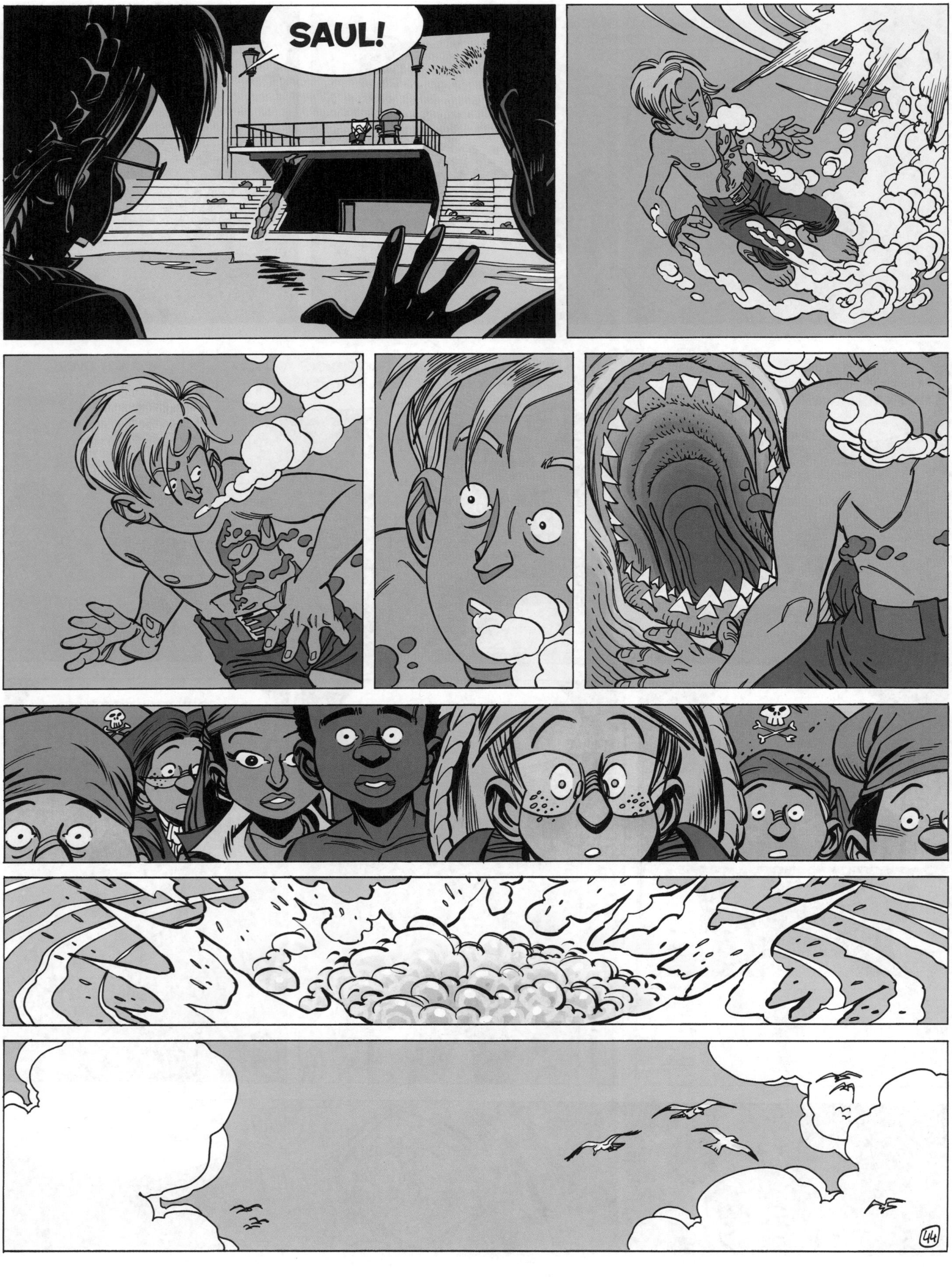
SAUL!
44

WELL? WHAT DOES HE WANT US TO DO?

YEAH, HE'S OUR NEW LEADER!

FIND YOUR OWN WAYS TO KEEP BUSY! DIDN'T YOU HEAR DODZI? HE DOESN'T WANT TO BE ANYONE'S LEADER.

...HE TOLD ME HE REMEMBERED WHAT HAPPENED.

THAT WHAT WAS HAPPENING TO US WAS... THE END OF THE WORLD, OR SOMETHING LIKE THAT.

THE END OF THE WORLD?

HE 'REMEMBERED'?... WHAT'S THAT SUPPOSED TO MEAN? THAT WE FORGOT WHAT HAPPENED?

WE WERE **ASLEEP!**

WELL, IVAN WASN'T. WHEN HE WAS ALL DRUNK, HE TOLD ME STUFF ABOUT HOW HIS DAD WOKE HIM UP!

I DID **WHAT?**

YEAH, YOU SAID SOMETHING ABOUT... ER... A GAME OF HAPPY FAMILY, I THINK.

TERRY! COME ON, THIS IS SERIOUS!

HEYYYY!?

NO, HE'S RIGHT... EXCEPT IT WAS THE *FIFTEEN FAMILIES*...

MY DAD SAID THAT... THE *FIFTEEN FAMILIES* WERE AFTER US AND THAT WE HAD TO LEAVE TOWN.

I'D COMPLETELY FORGOTTEN! IT'S UNBELIEVABLE!

DO YOU REMEMBER ANYTHING ELSE?

I... I HAVE TO GO BACK TO CAMPTON.

WHAT IS IT, IVAN?

...I THINK MY PARENTS WERE KILLED.

THESE REMEMBER FASTER THAN THE OTHERS, LITTLE SISTER.

YES.

THE CHILD WHO COULD DOOM US ALL IS PROBABLY WITH THEM...

...WE'LL GO WITH THEM.

COLOURS: CAROLINE & RALPH

FABIEN VEHLMANN BRUNO GAZZOTTI.